Why I think social conservatism is not logical

Table of contents

A. why I think it is not logical to be a social conservative

B. fiscal conservatism is ok sometimes but......

C. Why liberalism is the way

A.Why I think it is not logical to be a social conservative

I feel that social conservatives in the United states believe in ideals and situations that are " backward" in my opinion. A lot of them still have bigoted beliefs regarding minorities. Some of them are racists, they want segregation to come back. A number of them do not want gays to have equal rights and they believe in that there is a right way and a wrong way. They even have the belief that women stay at home ,and should not work or be into the military.There is no grey area with social conservatives as far as equal rights. Old fashioned yet bigoted beliefs is what social conservatives in the United states adhered to . This is why I think social conservatives are dangerous.

EQUAL PEOPLE
EQUAL RIGHTS
EQUAL LOVE

Gay rights are not
supported by social

conservatives. They tend to believe that marriage is between a man and a woman. This homophobia and other bigoted beliefs they have toward others who are perceived as " different" is the reason why I think social conservatism is not logical but a dangerous belief system designed to hurt others in the social sphere.

Coldness, cater to the rich

Many social conservatives care little for the poor or the disenfranchised.Many conservatives ,including Ronald Reagan regard the homeless as people who put themselves in that position . Their philosophy is very much the Marie Antoinette problem or more appropriate, the Donald trump problem- worried about being rich, getting rich and be cold to the poor. The term "let them eat cake" applies strongly with social conservatives.Worry about having a lavish lifestyle, or getting rich and being callous to the poor. While Marie Antoinette did not say those words reportedly

. The attitudes of many prominent social conservatives , and the republican party are very similar to the term " let them eat cake" , in other words, their policies and beliefs are callous to the poor.

Callous

Indifferent or insensitive to other people's feelings

I do not pay taxes, taxes are for the little people- Leona Helmsley

Callous (KAL uss)

- **Definition**: adj.- insensitive, having no feelings.
- **Synonyms**: heartless, unsympathetic
- **Link**: Callus

- Jack was so **callous** that he made fun of Mike's calluses in front of everyone in the locker room.
- A **callous** remark is a statement that does not take someone's feelings into consideration.
- It would be **callous** to be a millionaire and not ever donate any money to the poor.

Social conservatives are for the rich, restrict the rights of women and minorities , believe that gay marriage is wrong and believe that abortion is wrong ... the right to life.

courtesy of the internet

Social conservatives tend to believe that a woman does not have control of her body.They believe a baby uterus is life and that the law and courts must protect the unborn even to the

www.ingramcontent.com/pod-product-compliance
Lightning Source LLC
Chambersburg PA
CBHW021854170526
45157CB00006B/2441

threat of a woman's life. The social conservative ideology believes that the woman or the mother should not have no say or limited say on whether she should give birth to a child.

Some social conservatives believe that there are exceptions , for example ,the woman's life is in danger. Social conservatives believe in sexist viewpoints that a woman needs to stay

home and cook and
clean and be
subservient to the man
which is ridiculous and
ignorant.

SEXISM IS WRONG

DEFINITIONS OF SEXISM

Sexism
* Ideology that one gender is superior to another.

Sexual harassment
* Unwelcome sexualised comments, gestures &
physical contact. Includes offensive, humiliating,
intimidating or demeaning exchanges.

Sexual discrimination
* Excluding one gender from benefiting
from employment, services, communication
& civic participation.

STEMWomen.net

Courtesy by the internet

Racism

Some social conservatives think all African americans are dangerous, and they are all on welfare. This false belief and stereotypes is from ignorance and from a few cases. The truth is ,is that there are many African americans who are employed in many places. There are way more white americans who are on welfare because African americans are only 12 percent of the population which means that there are many more whites than blacks in this country. Also, while there are a disapportionate amount of blacks committing crimes, there are way more African American or black people not involved in any crimes. There are many social conservatives who are involved in fascist organizations like the KKK.Some members of the KKK and other radical racist groups call themselves "social conservatives". This factor is one reason why there are very few minorities and women ,gay people involved in social conservative causes like the republican party.

Trump and his ideology sometimes align itself with the ku klux klan

C. Why liberalism is the way

Liberalism, political doctrine that takes protecting and enhancing the freedom of the individual to be the central problem of politics. **Liberals** typically believe that government is necessary to protect individuals from being harmed by others, but they also recognize that government itself can pose a threat to ...

Liberalism is the belief that minorities and majority culture should have the same rights and freedoms. Things like sexism , racism and homophobia are considered illegal and discrimination to liberals .

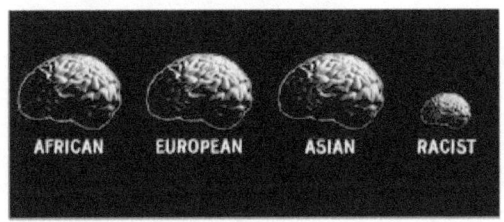